How to Get More 5 Star Reviews

Discover What Smart Business Owners Do to Get More Customers, Clients, & Patients from the Internet

By Mike LeMoine
©2019

Mike LeMoine

©2019 By Mike LeMoine
Published by Credibility Press
All rights reserved – ISBN 978-1090978493

What others say about working with Mike and his company: MaverickWebMarketing.com

Sue Pruett:

I've known Mike for several years, now, and found him and his team to be both trustworthy AND great at what they do! He's consulted with me on several occasions, and has helped my business tremendously. He's my go-to for all questions and challenges around internet marketing.

Jen:

We hired Maverick Web Marketing to produce a series of videos for our new website at Mednet and the entire experience was pleasant and professional. Their staff, in particular; Sean, Lori and Mike, were so helpful throughout the process. It can be a nerve-wracking task to be interviewed on camera, but they kept us calm and comfortable, and the end results were better than we expected. I highly recommend them if you need video assistance!

Brady Pofahl:
I have been working with Maverick Web Marketing for several years after going through bad experiences with other national legal marketing companies. I spent years trying to increase my client base and web presence but it seemed like every time a national company would complete their marketing and I would sign up for a large contract- they would proceed to forget about my website while still charging me thousands of dollars a month. I could not be happier that I went with Maverick and Mike LeMoine.

Mike has been nothing but straightforward and has developed my website, utilized his other marketing connections to help my business, managed ad campaigns, and gives me video updates about the performance of my website and the ads I am running. The most important part about my experience is that Mike has done everything he said he would do without asking me to sign a long-term contract. His performance has made it a long-term contract.

Dedication

Dedicated to my amazing wife Lori. You are my rock. You believed in me when I was just a firefighter chasing a dream of a better life for all of us.

You have endured (and continue to endure) the ups and downs of this entrepreneurial roller coaster. You have supported me and believed in me every step of the way.

None of this would ever be possible without you.

Mike LeMoine

About the Author

"Fireman" Mike LeMoine is one of the world's foremost experts on local business marketing. 15 years ago, Mike was a firefighter and paramedic who started selling on eBay to make extra money.

Never did he imagine that his small side hustle would eventually morph into a very successful digital marketing company (Maverick Web Marketing), gaining him national notoriety by helping local businesses become successful with his "maverick" marketing methods. His company has the most 5-Star Reviews in the state.

Mike gained national attention after he took over marketing for a few small businesses turning them into money making machines, while at the same time beating all the "marketing agencies" at their own game for a fraction of the budget.

He is two-time Amazon best-selling author who regularly speaks across the country teaching business owners how to use the internet to get more customers, clients, and patients.

Mike is also the host of Local Marketing Live which is New Mexico's largest small business marketing education event. Local Marketing Live is an exclusive monthly members-only event where small business owners from Albuquerque and the surrounding areas come to learn.

At Local Marketing Live Mike teaches actionable marketing strategies that can be implement right away to get more customers, clients, and patients! Members learn what's working now for small businesses in marketing so that they can make more money and grow their businesses!

Mike and his team are the brains behind many of the successful strategies that local businesses are using to get more customers, clients, and patients using his "maverick" ideas. Mike also teaches marketing agencies how to get results for their clients using smart internet marketing.

Mike is a committed husband to his wife Lori and together they are raising four great kids. If you are wondering, Mike no longer works for the fire department…but he will tell you that now as a small business owner, he puts out far more fires daily than he ever did when he was a firefighter!

Table of Contents

Introduction	11
Chapter 1 - The New Economy of Reputation and Relationships	15
Chapter 2 - Does My Online Reputation Really Matter?	23
Chapter 3 - You're Wasting All Your Money!	43
Chapter 4 - The Benefits of A 5-Star Reputation	55
Chapter 5 - The Most Important Piece of Your Marketing!	67
Chapter 6 - Awesome Messaging That Gets Results!	73
Chapter 7 - What Are They Saying Behind My Back?	85
Chapter 8 - Help! I Have A Negative Review (or Many Negatives)	91
Chapter 9 The Million Dollar Question	103
Chapter 10 - Getting People to Take Action	113
Chapter 11 - Where Do Reviews Need to Go Online?	123
Chapter 12 - Making Sure Your Team Is Up to Speed!	129
Chapter 13 - A Few Last Tips	135
Chapter 14 - The New Economy	145
The Wrap-Up	155

Mike LeMoine

Introduction

When I was younger, I applied to rent an apartment. Where it asked for references, I described my eBay feedback. To me, the best references I could show the apartment manager were the more than 1,000 people who had left me a 5-star review and said good things about me. I had a 100% feedback score and I was proud of it.

I also expected my feedback to "vouch" for my character.

The apartment manager looked at me obviously not knowing *what* to think. I explained that I sold on eBay and that up to that point, more than 3,000 people had done business with me without a problem. Additionally, over 1,000 of them went out of their way to say good things about me online. I explained that those reviews were all votes toward my character and that I could be trusted.

She said she had never seen anything like that on an apartment application, but she did agree and let me have the apartment based on my eBay character references! This was my first experience with the power of having a positive online reputation and I have never forgot that.

My story is pretty unique in the business world in that I a firefighter and paramedic. I was one of the youngest paramedics in the state. At that time, when you are a young paramedic, they put you with the experienced guys to "teach you the ropes."

I Needed More

I quickly learned that we often had down time after our daily commitments, and I needed to find something to do. Many people in my position would settle for video games, naps, and just hanging out. Those things did not work for me. I quickly decided I needed to find something productive to keep me busy.

I decided I would make money from the Internet. So, I began to teach myself how to do that. I started with eBay and then quickly began teaching myself all about Internet marketing. I wanted to know how to make it work.

It was not long after that I began helping some business owners with their online marketing and eventually was able to turn my knowledge into a business. I now own a digital marketing company – Maverick Web Marketing where we help businesses market online to bring them more customers, clients, and patients. Our work is so successful for local businesses that we have the most 5-Star Reviews in the state tons of client testimonial videos. You can see these on our website: MaverickWebMarketing.com

I am also fortunate to speak on the topic of online marketing for local businesses around the country. I am called on by many to help educate their audiences on the importance of online marketing for businesses and how to achieve success using the Internet.

I've never forgotten about my eBay days and the importance of owning a solid online reputation. As our business evolved, and as I had the opportunity to help more and more businesses, I recognized early how important online reviews were becoming for local businesses.

A Step Further

Once I realized how critical reviews can be, I began obsessing over all the aspects of online reviews. I studied all I could find out about maximizing online my ratings and reviews. I began helping businesses leverage my knowledge, and technology, to win online with reviews. This gave those businesses a positive reputation on the internet (A 5-Star Reputation) and as a result it brought them more business.

The game has changed drastically online. Today, 5-star reviews and a stellar reputation online is the most important thing that a business can do to market on the internet.

I applied my knowledge, our systems, and my efforts to many clients across a vast number of different industries. I am happy to report that those who listen are all winning in their industries when it comes to online reviews. Each of them has far more reviews than their competition and are being rewarded with new business because of it.

Your business can benefit the same way.

I wrote this book to help educate business owners about the importance of having a strong reputation online that is anchored with many 5-star reviews.

It is my hope that as you read this book, you will realize that the *most important* thing you can do for your business is to put systems in place to help bring in high online ratings and reviews. Not only to help you get more positive ratings and reviews, but I will show you how to turn them into world-class marketing success for your business as well!

The online world is changing so rapidly that those who "get this" will be so far ahead of their competition and they will be able to write their own ticket.

When I was a firefighter and paramedic, I wanted to help everyone I could. It is my sincere hope that this book will help you in your business and with your online marketing.

Chapter 1
The New Economy of Reputation and Relationships

Let me ask you a question. Have you heard of the company named Carfax? When I speak across the country and ask this question, almost 95% of the people in the room have heard of Carfax. There is a good reason for that. (It's okay if you haven't heard of them before because I am going to give you the full story now.)

Carfax is a service that basically gives you a "report card" for vehicles. They research past wrecks, performance problems, title history, and more for vehicles so that consumers might fully review a vehicle's true history before they make a buying decision.

Carfax knew that while their service was super-valuable to consumers, the average consumer only buys a car once every few years. That's no way to build a long-term sustainable business. Carfax also knew that in order to have a sustainable long-term business, they needed auto dealers to be their customers and not consumers. If they could get the dealers to subscribe to the service, then they would have customers for life across the country all paying every single month.

Carfax could have accomplished this goal in several different ways. The way they chose was simply brilliant. Instead of hiring a boatload of salesmen large enough to conquer the world, they just spent hundreds of millions of dollars each month on marketing to educate people (consumers). Their advertisements taught consumers to ask for a CarFax before you bought a car. They were on TV, they were on radio, they were in magazines, they were in newspapers, they were online.

They were all over the place!

Their message was simple; if a dealer could not provide you with a Carfax report, the dealer simply could not be trusted; therefore, neither could the vehicles the dealer sold. So (the implication went), if you could not get a Carfax you most likely would end up with a lemon. The bottom line was this: "Ask for a Carfax report and if they can't provide one, don't do business there. Instead, go to another dealer who can be trusted (and who provides CarFax reports)."

Of course, that caused potential car buyers across the country start going to the dealerships and asking for the CarFax. If the dealer didn't have a CarFax, they weren't getting the business. At this point CarFax basically backed every automobile dealer in the country into a corner saying, "You have to sign up for our CarFax service and provide it to your customers, or they're not going to trust you and you're not going to get their business."

BAAM!

At this point, the dealerships had no choice. They all signed up for Carfax. Continuing to ignore Carfax was not an option for them anymore. They knew that if they ignored Carfax (the standard their customers were judging them by), they would go out of business.

Why This Matters

This CarFax story is important because it directly relates to your business. The same thing that happened to auto dealers across the country with Carfax is now happening to you and your business. You see, collectively companies are spending hundreds of millions of dollars each month to educate consumers about one thing: Check the reviews, ratings, and the reputation of a business before you do business with it. The message is simple: If the business doesn't have good ratings and reviews, they can't be trusted, and you should not do business with them. The opposite goes for your business: strive for extremely positive ratings.

Companies like Google, Amazon, eBay, Angie's List, Yelp, Zomato, Tripadvisor, Yahoo, Bing, Yellow Pages, and many others are using their marketing dollars to plaster the message of "Reviews Matter" all over the place. Just like Carfax, they are online, they are on the radio airwaves, they are on TV, they are buying billboards, they are in magazines, they are all over the country educating consumers on how to evaluate your business before making a buying decision.

Much like the auto dealers were, you are now being backed into a corner and are faced with a problem that you simply can't ignore. Ignoring your reviews, ratings, and reputation is no longer an option for businesses that want to become or remain successful. Much like the dealers who ignored Carfax went out of business, many businesses who today choose to ignore their reviews, ratings, and reputation will no longer be in business in the future. I know this is not the news you wanted to hear, but if you are reading this book, you already have a sense of that. So, you are much further ahead than your competition who simply has no clue.

The New Economy

This world of reviews is exactly where the New Economy lives. This is the online environment that businesses are forced to operate in. It is the new way consumers are making buying decisions for themselves and their families. Businesses now must do more to make themselves trusted to the consumer. Businesses have to do everything they can to create the bond of trust with potential consumers if they want to be the one to get the customer. Operating a business in this new online economy is unlike anything you have ever faced before. For the first time in history, each and every one of your customers has a huge megaphone called the internet that allows them to freely broadcast their thoughts, experiences, and opinions of your business. It is because of this new economy that you must think differently, act differently, and do business differently.

This is Positive, Not a Bad Thing

Now look, I don't want to be all doom and gloom. After all, I am writing this book so you can educate yourself on systems, strategies, tactics, ideas, and methods to ensure that your business not only survives in the new economy of reputation and relationships but that it actually thrives. You are holding in your hands the answers you will need to successfully navigate this new online economy.

Throughout these pages, I am going to not only show you what to watch out for, but I am also going to show you what to do to ensure that your business becomes the most trusted business in your industry or category. If you follow the steps outlined in this book, you will welcome all the big-name companies that continually educating consumers about reviews because they will be driving new business to *you* every day for free!

We are living in exciting times as business owners, and those that choose to embrace the new way of doing business will forever reap the benefits.

At some level, you must know that what I am talking about is true. If you didn't, again, you would not still be holding this book. In the next chapter, I am going to present to you all the evidence that shows how your customers, clients, or patients are making decisions about businesses today. I am going to show you the most recent statistics to prove to you that ratings and reviews matter now more than ever for your business. I also break down to stats to really help you understand the meaning behind them so you can use them to make better decisions on how to market your business.

How to Get More 5-Star Reviews

More people speak out about what it's like to work with Mike and his company, MaverickWebMarketing.com

Val Romero:
Mike & his team at Maverick are ALL about helping the small business owner get better at selling their product or service. The entire team are experts at what they do. I appreciate Mike, his depth of knowledge, insights and willingness to share everything he knows to make your marketing rock. Thank you Maverick Web Marketing!

Diana Hakenholz, CMP, Director of Meetings and Education, Association of Collegiate Conference & Events Directors-International:
Mike Lemoine gave a valuable presentation to our members on the art and science of digital marketing for our business development educational forum. My attendees left with many ideas on how they can increase their online visibility. In addition, they were able to take away tools to evaluate

the effectiveness of their digital and understand the analytics.

Trey Cockrum:

Mike is a consistent deliverer of results for his clients. No beating around the bush. He doesn't take shortcuts and always values the success of his clients' businesses over his personal profit margins, which sets him apart in the digital marketing industry, and makes him easily the most attractive marketing agency in the state. He's been fantastic to work with, and I'm excited for you to get to work with him. If you're on the fence, take the plunge. You won't regret it in the slightest.

Chapter 2
Does My Online Reputation Really Matter?

I can hear you asking, "Why do I have to pay attention to this guy?" That's a great question because this is all new and we're in this new economy of reputation through relationships online.

Why does reputation marketing matter? Another fair question.

The way people are finding and evaluating your business online has changed. You must train your brain to accept that there is a new economy of reputation and relationships. The way you must conduct business is much different than before.

I will continue to hammer this point home throughout this book. If I can teach and show you about this new environment you are operating in, then you will have a much greater grasp and can make much better decisions regarding your business.

> **Warning:** I want to tell you that by reading this book you're gaining knowledge that almost every marketer or advertiser does not know. If

they did, they would for sure be doing things differently.

Don't Make a Move… Yet

I know that you are most likely getting hammered by people pitching you every service under the sun. They want to "help your business." They want you to "get you more customers, clients, or patients."

I want to warn you: Do not pay one more cent for anything until you read this chapter and chapter 3!

It is important that you understand this vital information before you spend any more money on marketing or advertising! I can promise you that you are being pitched by people who do not really understand what is at stake, and by paying them money you are increasing your chances of hurting your business. Again, I will explain this in detail in the next chapter, so you will have a full understanding of what I am talking about and can make smart decisions for your business.

The promise of this book is that I am going to help you discover what *smart business owners* are doing to get more customers from the internet.

The Research

One of the first things smart business owners do is ensure they are educated on what is happening online, how people are researching them, making decisions about them, and how people are finding them. I want you to have a full understanding of this information too.

How to Get More 5-Star Reviews

There has been a bunch of research, studies, and surveys that conducted around this. Let's break it down.

"A One-Star Increase in Yelp Rating Leads To A 5 to 9 Percent Increase In Revenue" (http://harvardmagazine.com/2011/10/hbs-study-finds-positive-yelp-reviews-lead-to-increased-business)

How would you like to give yourself an instant raise? In a study that was conducted by Harvard Business School, Assistant Professor Michael Luca found that, "A one-star increase in Yelp rating leads to a 5 to 9 percent increase in revenue." Smart business owners will use this data to their advantage and have systems in place to help drive more 5-Star reviews online for their business. They recognize that an increase in revenue is an increase in the bottom line.

They also know that the inverse is true as well. They know that losing stars in their ratings will cause them to lose money too. Therefore, they put systems in place that work to capture negative customer experiences before they are permanently tattooed online and hurting their business. They capture the reviews on their own private feedback pages and then work to resolve the problem long before the review is made public. I cover this more in Chapter 8 where we cover the psychology of negative online reviews and how to prevent them.

> "85% Of Consumers Trust Reviews as Much as a Personal Recommendation"
> (https://www.brightlocal.com/learn/local-consumer-review-survey-2017/)

This is a powerful statistic showing how important reviews are for your business. This applies to both positive and negative reviews too. There is a very important word in this statistic that most people miss. I bet you glanced over it as well, so I am going to point it out.

This data comes from *consumers* not just people looking online. Let's reread the information again: *"88% Of Consumers Trust Reviews as Much as a Personal Recommendation."*

This is powerful! It is not referring to people just shopping or looking. This is referring to buyers, to people who have pulled money out of their pocket and have given that money to a business.

Here is another stat for ya to consider:

> *91% of 18-34 year old consumers trust online reviews as much as personal recommendations.*

The "younger" generations are using reviews more and more to elevate local businesses and to make buying decisions. This stat shows that this new economy is not going anywhere. These "younger" generations are not going to change their ways.

This means that they person who is 32 today and looks at reviews will still do so when they are 42, 52, or 62. We will continue to see more and more people using reviews as a decision mechanism of where to spend their dollars.

Also, I would have you consider that young kids are

influencing where their parents spend money too. So far we have just talked about adults…but what about the kids. How in the world would they come into play here?

Well, let me tell you a story that repeats itself several times a month in my own family.

When we are out and about trying to decide where to eat or what to do our kids pull out their phones and start "Googling."

"This place looks good…oh wait, they only have 4 starts…never mind."

And with that statement a local business that could have had the opportunity to serve our family just lost out. They lost out on a customer because my nine year old looked at reviews and basically said…we can't go there…and you know what *no one* disagreed with him.

As a result whatever business he was looking at lost out on between $60 to $100 which is the average of what it takes to feed my family of six when we eat out.

Now, let me ask you a question…My nine-year-old with a smart phone is influencing where I spend my dollars. Do you think he is going to change his ways as he gets older? No!

In fact, I would guess that he will trust reviews and they will influence him even more. So, when he gets to an age where he is making his own decisions for him and his family…if your business has not changed its way…well…then you will lose his business too.

Do you see why this new economy of reputation and relationships is *so* important? I really hope you do. Those that "get it" will thrive. Those who don't…well maybe the 3 or 4 people who use the yellow pages will be enough to keep you in business….my guess however is that those who do not embrace this new way of thinking will go out of business because they will be starving for revenue as people choose to spend their hard earned dollars somewhere else…a place they trust because of 5-Star Reviews!

If Disaster Struck…

Let me ask you something. If you were to lose 85% to 91% of your buyers, can you survive on the 15% to 9% of customers you have left? If not, you better be prepared to make this topic a very important one for your business because most consumers who are going to spend money are looking at reviews and ratings of businesses.

Every business owner I talk to tells me that *word of mouth* or *referrals* is the best form of advertising for them. In the new economy of reputation and relationships, online ratings and reviews are the *new word of mouth marketing*.

I talk more about this later in the book.

The Trust Factor

"73% Of Consumers Say That Positive Reviews Make Them Trust a Local Business More" (https://www.brightlocal.com/learn/local-consumer-review-survey-2017/)

You and I both know that people doing business with us revolves around trust. You will hear a lot of people quote the overused cliché, "Know, Like, and Trust." The biggest of these is *trust*.

Let me give you an example. Did you know the pilot who flew the last plane you were on? Most likely not. Did you like the pilot? You did once you landed, but again you most likely did not know him or her. Did you trust the pilot? Of course, you did, or you would have never gotten on that plane in a million years!

People who are going to become your customers, clients, or patients will do so because they trust you. This stat proves that people trust a business more that has positive reviews.

If we just use our street smarts here, then we can learn an important lesson. That lesson is that if you have more positive reviews you will be more trusted. If you are more trusted, you will get more customers, clients, or patients in your door because for 73% of people, this is a major decision-making factor.

> **Note:** A big thing that almost no one talks about is the fact that to be successful in this new economy, you can't just focus on getting 5-Star reviews. You must also have a way to avoid getting negative reviews too because any negative review can directly affect your ability to get new clients and therefore affect your revenue too!

Getting the Reviews

I can sense your frustration and I assure you that you are not alone. As I share this statistic with clients, they inevitably all tell me some version of the same thing: "Mike, I know that more reviews are going to equal more business, that's a no brainer…But tell me *how* I get more 5 Star reviews!"

Don't worry. I am going to tell you how. It may disappoint you to know that there is no one trick, hack, or secret to getting more positive reviews. I know that comes as a big surprise especially as people in my industry are preaching that they have the silver bullet, or golden nuggets, or a lucky rabbit's foot, or whatever other thing they are pitching this week to get you to pay them money.

The real way to get more 5-Star reviews for your business is to have a solid system with many pieces working for you at all times. All our clients who follow our teaching and systems have the most 5-Star reviews in their industry! Yes, I will be teaching you about the system, that is why I wrote this book for you.

"85% of Consumers Say They Read up to 10 Reviews" (http://www.brightlocal.com/2014/07/01/local-consumer-review-survey-2014/)

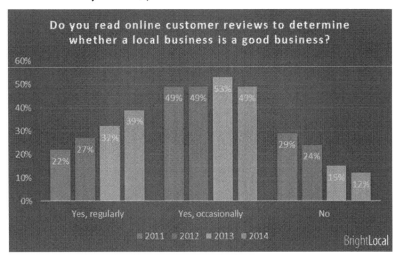

With 85% of people reading up to 10 reviews, you know what that means right? It means that your business needs to have at least 10 positive reviews online so that you can be viewed as trusted.

This also does not mean *only* 10 reviews! It actually means 10 recent reviews, because review sites post reviews in the order they come in. If you have a negative rating as part of the first 10 that people see, you might as well not even have the positives there because people are going to home in on the negative one.

That means you must have a steady stream of positive reviews coming in online. I will say this many times in this book: "The best defense against negative reviews is a positive offense!"

Reviews Produce Action

> "72% Of Consumers Will Take Action After Reading A Positive Review" (http://www.brightlocal.com/2014/07/01/local-consumer-review-survey-2014/)

(Figure follows on next page.)

Inside of this 72% stat from Bright Local are some very interesting numbers.

That 72% is divided into two clear actions:

- 57% say they will visit the business' website after reading the review.
- 15% say they will phone the business up after reading the review.

7 out of 10 people who read positive reviews will take some sort of positive action afterwards. Again, this just goes to show how important positive reviews are

for your business. Additionally, people who are reading reviews are narrowing down on who they are going to do business with. These types of people are much closer to making a decision on who to do business with.

The positive reviews they are reading about you (or the lack of positive reviews) will play a major role in your ability to turn them from a searcher into a customer, client, or patient. This has a direct impact on your bottom line.

> "92% of Users Will Use a Local Business If It Has a 4-Star Rating" (http://www.brightlocal.com/2014/07/01/local-consumer-review-survey-2014/)

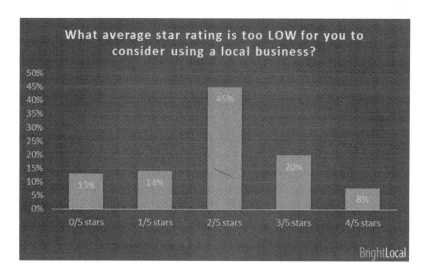

This stat is one that excites me. Here's why: It is almost impossible for a business that has any volume of customers, clients, or patients to have a perfect 5-Star online review 100% of the time. Despite all the systems we have in place to try and prevent negatives from going online and to promote positives online, inevitability you will get a bad review from time to time that will drop your rating for a little bit.

The good news is that it won't affect you that much as long as you have a 4-star or above rating.

I hope you can begin to understand why we are so adamant about getting as many 5-Star online reviews for your business as possible. It is because we know that if you have a bunch of 5-Star reviews and then you get a negative review the impact is minimal. Compare that to the business that has zero to a few stars. They are one review away from having a negative reputation online.

This is so important to understand that we dedicated an entire chapter to it. You can read about this in the chapter called "Review Insurance."

We've Always Done It This Way

This is the last statistic I want to leave you with. So many businesses are locked into the old way of doing things because they tell me, "This is what we have always done, and it seems to work okay."

I always wonder, do they just want to do "okay" in business or do they want to do great?

Also, with the way the internet is moving and the way our consumers are finding businesses, it is only a matter of time before the businesses who are stuck in the old way of doing things will be wiped out by an upstart and motivated competitor who understands this new economy of reputation and relationships.

This graphic comes from Nielsen.

To What Extent Do You Trust The Following Forms Of Advertising?

	Trust Completely/ Somewhat	Don't Trust Much/ At All
Recommendations from people I know	92%	8%
Consumer opinions posted online	70%	30%
Editorial content such as newspaper articles	58%	42%
Branded Websites	58%	42%
Emails I signed up for	50%	50%
Ads on TV	47%	53%
Display ads on mobile devices	33%	67%
Text ads on mobile phones	29%	71%

Source: Nielsen Global Trust in Advertising Survey, Q3 2011

They are the same company that survey's people to see what you are watching on TV.

As you can see "personal recommendations from people I know" is the top ranked as far as trust goes. Did you see what is the next most trusted form of advertising? "Consumer opinions posted online"! Here's what is crazy: People trust opinions from a stranger more than they trust any other form of marketing or advertising!

Think about this... Look up there. Look at all the different kinds of marketing and media you have most likely paid for. Do you have a website? Most likely you do. Having a website is important, but not as important as making sure that ratings and reviews about your business online are positive. We can go line by line, but I won't waste your time.

The bottom line is this: Smart businesses owners understand this graphic and they invest into making sure that their online rating, reviews, and reputation is in tip-top shape before they spend money on other things.

They understand that consumer opinions online are the closest thing they can get to the old-style word of mouth advertising, and they know that having positive ratings and reviews will bring them the biggest return on their investment because it is the most trusted form of advertising, outside of personal recommendations.

Just to remind you, we have dedicated a whole chapter towards explaining how doing other forms of marketing before making sure your ratings and reviews are solid is a very bad business strategy that can hurt you big time!

If you're like me, this chapter with all these stats is not the most fun. You are holding a book about how to get more 5-Star reviews and you want to get to that meat of it.

You don't need stats to tell you how important it is, you're living it every day. I can appreciate your enthusiasm! However, in order to stay credible, I have to back up my talk with stats. I don't want to be like every other person out there who calls himself or herself an expert and spews poisonous advice. I want to show you credible data and back it up with my knowledge so you understand how important this is to your business. After all, my own credibility and trust is on the line with you with every sentence of this book you read. I know how important that is! Hence why we show statistics and not just blow hot air around here.

Going Forward

Okay, you made it through the toughest chapter in the book! The next chapter pisses a lot of people off (maybe even you). People get mad for various reasons. Some because they realize they have been taken for a ride by unsavvy, inept marketers and others because they are marketers and the chapter blows a giant hole in everything they are trying to sell to unsuspecting businesses.

My job is to educate you based on my knowledge and I hope that if you do get upset that you don't "shoot the messenger" because the good thing is you can change it!

More people speak out about what it's like to work with Mike and his company, MaverickWebMarketing.com

Tobias Lucero:
Very professional and knowledgeable staff! They helped get my company's name spread across the country and now we have several overseas customers purchasing products from us in New Mexico!

Yvonne Duran:
Absolutely the most informative and helpful resource for business knowledge available at such a convenient venue.... the web short clips have been influential and formative. I cannot thank Mike enough and his team for sharing such great tips and helping me see such improvement in my business experience.

Daniel Leake:
The Maverick team produced helped me create several dozen videos to use on my website. It was clear they had thought through every detail and

made the couple days of shooting so so simple for me.

The team is kind and professional.

We recorded several dozen videos then their team gave me edited versions quickly that look great. I'm very happy I went with Maverick.

Plus –they were able to do some other graphics work for me that turned out awesome!

I'll definitely be calling them again for my next project.

Mike LeMoine

Chapter 3
You're Wasting All Your Money!

I said at the end of the previous chapter that this chapter is one that upsets some people. I can live with this. Our mission is to help small businesses, so if I piss some people off in the process of accomplishing my mission…well, I'm ok with it. When I was working as a fire fighter and paramedic, many times I had to be the person who was not the most popular one. I had to make decisions and tell people "how things were" whether they wanted to hear them or not.

Let me tell you something. If you are not focusing on your online reputation and generating 5-star reviews for your business, *all other* forms of marketing and advertising are doing you horrible disservice!

I talk to many business owners who are shelling out hundreds to thousands of dollars a month on SEO or search engine optimization. They are attempting to get their business ranked higher in Google.

On the surface, this seems innocent enough right? They (or you) want to be visible to people searching so that they can get more business. That's all well and good except for one problem.

If you are spending money on search engine optimization and you are not working to build a solid 5-star reputation at the same time or before you start, what happens when you get a negative review?

SEO at the Expense of Reviews

Let me tell you what happens. If you are paying money each month for SEO and you are not protecting your reputation, you will end up paying to advertise your negative review(s) to the world.

You pay month after month to get to the top (if the people you hired actually keep their word) and then that negative review hits and now you are at the top showcasing a negative reputation to the world! And there is nothing you can do about it. So, you just spent tens of thousands of dollars to advertise your negative reputation, *YIKES!*

See, this is why we preach to anyone who will listen that building a solid 5-star reputation is an absolute must if you are doing any type of SEO. Even if you do it alongside SEO, that is fine, but you must have a system in place to protect you from being at the top of Google with negative reviews!

A mistake like that could cripple your business for good! Now, let me talk about the other forms of advertising too.

Look at ads you are running or just look around. Everyone is putting their website all over the place. Radio,

TV, Newspapers, Magazines, Billboards, Yellow Pages, and so on.

Everyone (most likely you too) wants people to go to their website. However, that does not really happen. Let me teach you how people find local businesses after they hear or see an ad.

They go into Google and they type in the business name and the city that the business is in. That is how they find businesses they are looking for… even if they came from an ad.

The Four Major Shifts

There are Four Major Shifts that have happened online that affect you as a business owner. You must be aware of these shifts because if you are not then every penny you are currently spending on marketing and advertising is hurting you and your business or has great potential to.

Major Online Shift #1:

You don't usually remember the business's Web address. You remember the business's name.

The first major change that has happened online is if you go into Google and you put in your business name and your city, instantly that pulls up your company's reputation. This is your businesses report card online.

What does it show you right there? If you have more than five reviews, it shows the stars. It's instantly clear to people if your business can be trusted…or not!

If you don't have a good reputation online, it shows instantly. It's an instant report card on your business, and anyone can see it.

Stop what you are doing right now and type your business name and your city into Google and hit enter.

What do you see?

In most cases it will be your online report card from Google. You will either see no reviews (bad), negative reviews (really bad), a few positive reviews (not that helpful), or a 5-star reputation (awesome!).

> **Note:** If you are one of the ones that has the solid 5-Star reputation online right now you better ask yourself what system do you have in place to protect and grow that reputation? Your competitors will be catching on sooner or later, and you want to make sure you stay way ahead of the pack.

This is the exact reason you have to reevaluate all your marketing and advertising you are currently doing. Are you driving people to see no reputation, or worse a negative reputation?

One of the quickest ways some of our clients instantly increase the value of their advertising is by working with us to get them more 5-star reviews online. This way when people are searching from their ads, they see a 5-star reputation. This instantly makes all their other marketing and advertising more valuable.

Many times, you're locked into a contract for ads. Sometimes it can be for six months to a year. The best thing you can do is invest alongside that to increase your reviews online. This will ensure that your ad campaign that you are locked into can give you the biggest return on your investment.

Think about it, if you are going to advertise don't you want people seeing a positive 5-star reviewing when they research your business?

Of course, you do!

Major Online Shift #2:

Reviews are a major factor in all rankings on the search engines now, whether it's Google, Yahoo, or Bing.

Reviews matter.

Even on YouTube, a video that gets more thumbs up and more comments is going to show up in search engines more than a video that gets no reviews.

This is where reviews play a major role: they affect Google and the way everything ranks. Google's algorithms look at your Google My Business page, it looks at the number of reviews you have, it looks at your Website, and it ties all these things together.

What we have found is that businesses that have more positive reviews and 5-star reputations tend to rise higher in the search engines than businesses that don't. It Makes sense really.

Google and other search engines want their customers (the searchers) to find what they are looking for. If someone is searching for a local business, then they want that person to find a reputable business that will take care of them and give them great service.

Since none of them have the man power to go do surveys and inspections of all the local businesses in the world, they rely on ratings and reviews to help them review businesses and to help decided what businesses they show in their searches. So, the more positive ratings and reviews you have the more you will be rewarded with good placement over time in the search engines.

Major Online Shift #3:
Your businesses reputation is attached to it in all major areas of Google and the internet.

In Google Maps, your reputation shows up right next to your business. Why does that matter?

Because people use Google Maps to find the location of your business. If someone has made a decision to do business with you and they put your information into Google maps to go find you and they see you have a bad reputation, they'll look elsewhere.

We can't let that happen.

That's another reason why reviews and your reputation matter so much. I talked just a little bit ago about Google My Business, but Google now screens your reviews against your Website and all the information on there and it helps determine ranking placement for local businesses.

Again, if your Website is the same as somebody else's, but one company has great reviews, they have a 5-star reputation and you don't, that company is going to actually rank higher than you most times in the search engines based on their reviews.

What about local directories you say? Excellent question. There's no shortage of directories a local business can be in. It's hard for business owners to be able to keep up with local directories, but they're out there.

They're under the names of City Search, Manta, Local.com, Super Pages, Yellow Pages, and many more, thousands actually. There's a plethora of these directories, and reviews matter in these directories too, for two reasons:

Number one, a subset of your prospective customers, patients, and clients use those to find local businesses, so you want to have a good review there.

Number two, a lot of times, those directories can actually rank in the search engines (especially after recent Google updates). If it's ranking in the search engines and it's showing a negative review, then when somebody does a Google search looking for your product or service, they're going to instantly see your business has a negative review.

That's why reputation marketing matters to your business. Again, it's just that yardstick of quality. You have to be paying attention to your online reputation and your reputation marketing for that reason.

Major Online Shift #4:
Reviews send you pre-qualified customers.

Let's recap the stats one more time just to prove the point that if you have a 5-Star rating and reputation online you will get prequalified customers ready to buy.

Remember, 85 percent of people trust reviews as much as personal recommendations. If you take this a step further, BriteLocal reports that most people look for six to ten reviews on the Internet, six to ten positive reviews on the Internet, before they make a buying decision.

97 percent of people looking for a business read those reviews. Let's look at the six to ten 5-star reviews you need to have.

What's happening is, if you don't have six to ten 5-star reviews, your business is viewed as not trusted online. Whether you deserve that reputation or not.

This chapter is meant to serve as a bit of a wake-up call to you. I want you to look at how you are currently spending your money on marketing and advertising. How are you spending your money to market your business online?

If you are not doing something to be working towards a 5-Star reputation online each and every day chances are you are wasting your time and money, or at least not getting the greatest return…

Worse, you are going to find yourself out tens of thousands of dollars and realize you have just paid a ton of money to showcase your bad reputation online if someone hits you with a negative review that you are not prepared for.

The bottom line is in this new economy you must have a system in place to constantly be working to get you real reviews from real customers on a continual basis. This will help strengthen all your marketing and advertising, it will bring you new customers, help you rank higher in Google, and it will also protect you if you get hit with a negative review too!

More people speak out about what it's like to work with Mike and his company, MaverickWebMarketing.com

★★★★★

Rob Weinstein:

Few people have an outstanding knowledge of marketing and also a proven track record of measurable success. Mike LeMoine has both. He's a fountain of knowledge and he has a proven track record that's quite impressive.

I've heard many people spout off about the latest marketing approaches but I always question if they have ever successfully marketed anything other than info on "how to market."

It's the same feeling I got in college when listening to college professors talking about business and questioning if they've ever actually been in the trenches and had any actual success or if they were just preaching "theory."

I have been lucky enough to know Mike LeMoine as a colleague in mastermind groups and as his customer for the past 5 years.

Mike has been responsible for scripting and producing sales videos, he's helped with our website sales conversions, his team manages our Adwords and even produces a weekly YouTube video channel for my company. He's even helped at our national conferences on multiple levels and handles our social media advertising. In short, Mike has built an amazing turnkey marketing factory that's second to none.

If you need help implementing marketing or need someone that can do it for you, there is no one better qualified than Mike and his company maverick web marketing.

I'm also very excited that he's taking the reigns at PowerCircle. He's a perfect fit and a huge asset to companies that can participate.

Justin Poff:
Awesome people to work with. Always full of good ideas and there to help you when toy need it!!

Stacy Blackwell:
I worked with Jesse and he was amazing every step of the process. From explaining the project to how to see the final product, their customer service was incredible. The product was incredible too, but the help along the way made me a believer!

Chapter 4
The Benefits of a 5-Star Reputation

So, you may be asking, "If I'm going to put all this effort into reviews, how does it benefit my marketing in real life?"

Well for starters, there is a good chance your business is going to show up higher in the search engines with multiple 5-star reviews. That's huge because people are making buying decisions on that every day.

Chances are, if you're reading this book early enough and taking action, you're going to notice that most of your competitors aren't paying attention to this at all. It's going to put you out ahead of your competition.

Many of my clients who have listened to me and trusted me got started on their reviews years ago. Now, they have the *most* 5-star reviews and their competition will never catch them. They dominate and lead their industries and charge much more for their services. I would highly encourage you to contact me if you are not winning online in the review game. I can help you and your business just like I have helped all my other clients!

You're going to be able to build up a 5-star reputation, get those 5-star reviews next to your business, and be able to blow out your competition before they even *realize* that this matters!

Another way it benefits you is that it drives pre-qualified traffic. It's going to send pre-qualified customers who are looking to spend money. We talked about that in the last chapter in detail.

Pricing Considerations

Here's what we know: a customer who is looking for quality doesn't care about price that much.

As you get a 5-star reputation on the Internet, you're going to be able to increase your prices and be able to get higher profit margins, just based on having that 5-star reputation. When it comes down to it, people would rather have quality over low priced mediocre services in most instances.

If a customer, client, or patient only cares about price - that's not the type of customer you want anyway. You want a customer who is going to invest in your products and services because of the quality, not because you have the cheapest prices.

By having great margins, you will then be able to over-deliver, give unmatched value, and have a customer for life. These customers will be happy with your service, and happy to give you great feedback. Thus, repeating the cycle!

Spread the Good Word

Did I mention to you that you could use it on other parts of your business? You can then take those 5-star reviews and put them on your website. When visitors are on your site and they start thinking about making that buying decision or visiting your business, they see your 5-star reviews all over your website. This gives you instant credibility and trust. Again, you're using social proof in marketing. You take those reviews and put them all over your website and you're able to attract the right type of customer.

You take these reviews and you put them on postcards if you're doing direct mail. You put them in your newspaper ads, in the phonebook, your Yellow Pages ad, your billboard, you talk about them on the radio, show them on TV commercials, anywhere you are marketing your business you can leverage those reviews.

This is what real people are saying about you. And it needs to be seen my friends! When you have evidence and proof of real people saying great things about your business, you want to exploit that. You want to use it absolutely everywhere.

Let's talk about using 5-star reviews on YouTube. Let me give you some ideas here. Number one, you can take a screenshot of that review and have a voice-over read that review.

Here's an example:

> "Hey, this Mike from Maverick. This 5-star review just came in for us. Please allow me to read to you what Bonnie said."

Then you read the review and say, "We're so grateful to Bonnie for leaving us this kind review. If you want to be our next happy customer, go visit us here."

If you were to do four of those videos a month and put them on YouTube where you read customer reviews, after just a few months, you have a bunch of videos on YouTube working for you, showing what happy customers said. That's another way to be able to use these 5-star reviews.

> **Note:** Customer on our reputation marketing program enjoy professional high-quality videos made for their reviews each month. We will talk more about that in a later chapter.

Maverick Web Marketing's Case Example

I'd like to share a phenomenal story from my company, *Maverick Web Marketing*.

We put together an ad for a local painter. We completely revamped the ad from anything he had ever done before. For the headline of his ad we put, "Albuquerque's Five-Star House Painter."

We included his phone number, we put a picture of his van, and we added a ton of screen shots of reviews people had left him.

The great thing was I didn't have to put in his ad that he painted houses, that he painted buildings, that he painted commercial structures, that he painted interior or exterior.

People already knew that. He's a painter.

What they didn't know was if this guy does quality work. We were able to show through using reputation marketing that he absolutely does.

The ad was very well received. This is an ad that normally wouldn't have received that kind of traction, but because we did that, we attracted a new type of customer because we showcased his reputation.

5 Stars Are Visual

Just in case you need another reason why reputation marketing can benefit your marketing: it's visual.

When you put those 5-stars above that review or below that review, it catches people's eyes. People know what 5-stars means.

Five stars mean quality, professionalism, excellent service. Five stars mean people don't have to worry about getting ripped off.

People don't have to worry about crappy work, people can let them into their homes, they can let them work on their mouths if they're dentists, they can let them work on your back if they're chiropractors. It means people can trust this person to do the job and do it well.

Five stars says so much. You've heard the saying, "A picture is worth a thousand words." Those 5-stars tell somebody more about your business than you ever could.

If you only have one of the 5-stars, believe me, that tells a story as well. If you don't have a great reputation on the Internet, people will not take a chance on you.

Remember the statistic about people trusting reviews as much as recommendations from a friend? If you have bad reviews, they will look at those reviews, trust them, and drive right past your business.

They want to see what people said about your business. If you have a great 5-star reputation you will get noticed. Reviews are so visual, you're going to be able to capture more traffic, convert more people and have more people trust you. This isn't for everybody, but another reason having those 5-star reviews is bragging rights. We're all in business and we're in business to make money, but we all have competitors. If you can build a great 5-star reputation and your competitors can't, that gives you bragging rights in your industry.

Why it Matters Most

But let's cut to the chase now, the real reason why it matters to you: if you have that 5-star reputation, you are viewed as the authority and the expert in your industry. You are the person people go to so they can get their problems solved! If you have a bunch of 5-star reviews, they know that you have happy customers.

And as if you needed another reason… what the heck! The last way that you can benefit from 5-star reviews is that when you are the expert and authority and you get out ahead of the pack, it's going to be very hard for your competition to catch you.

When we do video marketing, the first person to use video usually will dominate the industry. It's the same thing with reputation marketing: the first person to really embrace reputation marketing and follow the things I'm talking about here will usually dominate their industry with a positive 5-star reputation, and it's going to be very difficult for their competitors to catch them.

That's what I'm talking about. I just hope that you're on the ball, get this, and start the hard process now, so you can enjoy the benefits of being an industry leader because you have a great reputation online.

Mike LeMoine

More people speak out about what it's like to work with Mike and his company, MaverickWebMarketing.com

The Extra Mile Gift Shop:
  I had the opportunity to speak with Mike LeMoine today. I wanted to discuss some marketing strategies I would like to use for some potential clients in a very specific industry. I went into the call with a very good strategy and came out of the call with an even better one!

  I value Mike's suggestions very highly and would not hesitate to call him again if I wanted to bounce something off of someone in this industry. He is extremely knowledgeable and stays in touch with what ACTUALLY works, not just what SHOULD work. When marketers need marketing consulting, this is the guy they call and if you want to stretch every marketing dollar your business spends as far as it will go, I'd call Mike.

Nancy Alexander:
We filmed some instructional, how-to videos in my studio. I wanted these videos to really look professional. They needed an introduction and several other elements throughout. I am amazed that they look so professional! Maverick Web Marketing did an excellent job and I look forward to using them again!

Steven Simpson, President, Total Asset Managers LLC:
Maverick has been very instrumental in the success of our business. They have taken our visibility and outreach to a level that I didn't think was possible! From website development to video production, we would absolutely not be where we are at without them. We owe a major facet of our success to Maverick. They have our absolute highest recommendation possible. Thank you Maverick to paving our road to success!

Tammy Byrd, Total Asset Managers, LLC:
Maverick Web Marketing built an awesome website for us. They listened to us and created a masterpiece that far exceeded our expectations. Their ongoing support is of the greatest value to us. They are responsive, easy to communicate with and understand, and are very customer satisfaction driven. We have asked them to incorporate a few features and functions to our web-site that are custom to our business model and they provided an

end result as if they had done it a thousand times before. If there was a 6th and 7th star I could give them, I would. This is one company you will not be sorry you invested with!

Mike LeMoine

Chapter 5
The Most Important Piece of Your Marketing!

People ask me all the time, "What is the most important piece of marketing?" One of the things you've got to understand is that when you're looking at marketing, the absolute most important part of marketing is the message. So many people think it's what we call at Maverick, "The Medium." Let me just go through the difference between the two with you.

The medium is usually what people are buying. They get confused a lot of times between the medium and the message. Medium is how the message is delivered. TV is a medium. TV delivers content via screen with words and pictures, but TV is the medium. Radio delivers the message; it's the medium that delivers sound. Newspapers, Yellow Pages, Magazines: those are the mediums that deliver words and pictures and visual things to people.

The paper is a medium. The billboard is the medium that puts information in front of people. The most important part of marketing is not the medium. It's the *message*.

So many people get that confused. Let me tell you, when you "buy" marketing and you're going to buy a *medium* (it doesn't matter if it's TV, newspapers, billboards or whatever), here's what usually happens; you're paying for the cost of the media. Then what happens is they'll create the ad for you for free. *Yay!* Just what you wanted right? An ad created for free by a sales person who does not really get how to market the right way.

If you're somebody who has never paid for the message to be created, but you've always just paid for the medium, this might be why your advertising is not as effective as you would like it to be. It's usually because you get what you pay for. Imagine that.

Unless you're paying a professional to develop the *most important* part of your advertising, *the message*, you're just not going to get very far. Remember this is a marathon, not a sprint.

Creating a cheap, ineffective message to throw something out there in the world isn't going to make a difference in the short or long run. It's a million times better to create a quality, tested, and meaningful message.

Everybody out there calls themselves a marketing consultant. Even the guy who sells advertising on the back of a grocery receipt calls himself a marketing consultant. I'm even pretty sure I heard my friend's dog say just the other day he was a marketing consultant.

But it doesn't work that way! A true marketing consultant is somebody who's going to take your business and help craft the message. They're going to test the message. Once you have a working message, they're going to help you select the media that will reach the right market.

So, to have an effective ad you really need 3 parts:

- Market
- Message
- Media

While these are three vital parts of your marketing, the messaging is where you can make a huge difference in the quality of your ads.

Okay, now that I you understand that the most important piece of marketing is the message, I am going to teach you a great way to get the absolute best "messaging" for your ads.

In the next chapter I am going to teach you all about how to use your 5-star ratings and reviews to create awesome messaging for all your marketing.

Mike LeMoine

More people speak out about what it's like to work with Mike and his company, MaverickWebMarketing.com

Kathleen Rhodes:

I was impressed by "Fireman Mike's" video about the ease of using Google Apps for email. It's something I had tried to set up on my own, without success. I ended up working with Sean Fonseca at Maverick Web Marketing, who not only set it up but also provided some screencast videos to walk me through the next steps. I can't say enough positive things about these guys! I expect to refer some colleagues to them soon.

Tamela Lewis, Smart and Heart:

Mike's willingness to engage in a discussion and his ability to listen was one of the best demonstrated skills I have seen in twenty years of business. Incredibly impressive. He was honest in his evaluation of what MWM could do for my business. His input was thorough, knowledgeable, and accurate. Very astute. And greatly appreciated.

Audrey Joubert:

Maverick has helped our business all the way over here in Zimbabwe, Africa to start turning around! Their team is amazing to work with! They have never let the distance get in the way of producing outstanding results for our marketing. A huge thank you to all you guys at Maverick.

If you are wanting to get your business in front of the right audience, with the right message, I would recommend Maverick without a doubt!

Tim Fahndrich:

I love working with Mike and his team. Not only are they really smart about internet marketing and video, but they really over-deliver on their products and services. I recently had the opportunity to begin working with Maverick on a system they had put together and I have been very pleased with the results that we get on a regular basis because of it. Thank you Mike and team.

Chapter 6
Awesome Messaging That Gets Results!

Here's the real scoop folks: once you have a message that works, the medium doesn't really matter because the message works. You can now deliver a good congruent working message via any medium and you're going to have success as long as the medium helps you reach your market.

Most people do this all wrong. When we talk about the most important part of advertising and marketing, we're really talking about the message.

Why does that matter in reputation marketing? Most advertising is damn boring. That's why nobody responds to it. Advertising is boring. Ads are boring. They suck.

The reason why they suck so bad is because of platitudes. What are platitudes? Platitudes are things in your marketing that are boring. Things that people are saying over and over that lack real meaning.

Rich Harshaw, a marketing genius, defines a platitude like this: "Platitudes are words or phrases that are drearily commonplace and predictable, that lack power to invoke interest through overuse or repetition that nevertheless are stated as though they were original or significant."

The Evaluation Test

When we think of platitudes, we have a three-part platitude evaluation test.

The first one is the "Well, I would hope so" test. This test is all around the messaging, which is the most important part of marketing. What we mean by this is if you look at marketing in advertising, what you'll see is the auto body guy who says, "We fix dings and dents." What do we say? "I should hope so; you're an auto body guy."

It's the windshield repair guy who says, "I fix cracked windshields." I would hope so. That's what you do. You're the windshield repair guy.

Or a chiropractor who says, "I help heal your hurt back." I would hope so. You're a chiropractor. I don't want to see an ad for a chiropractor that says, "I'm going to make your back worse. Come in here and you're going to leave more crooked than when you walked in." Of course not!

Or the dentist who says, "I'm going to give you a beautiful smile." I would hope so. You're a dentist. That's kind of what your job is.

So many people do this in their marketing and advertising and it's kind of funny. So many people do this, and they think that what they're saying is important, when in reality what they're saying is really not important at all. Their ad instantly seems boring. *Maestro, cue the elevator music!*

The second platitude evaluation is, "Who else can say that?" It's similar to the first one, but it's occurred usually because of all the ad agencies and brand builders. The question is not, "Who else can do what you do?" but "Who else can say what you say?" The answer is usually anybody and everybody. Whether it's true or not.

Let me give you an example. How about the chiropractor who says, "I've been in business 25 years," while the ad from his competitor goes, "In practice 20 years?" It doesn't matter. Who else can say that? Everybody can usually say what you're saying. It doesn't matter if they can do what you do. You look at so many ads out there and everybody is saying they do the same thing. Again, it's not about who can do what you do, it's who can say what you say?

Everyone can do that, so it makes ads very boring. They don't stand out. They're boring. They're plain. They don't invoke any emotion.

If we look at platitudes, they are words or phrases that are very commonplace and predictable that lack the power to provoke interest through overuse or repetition that nevertheless are stated as though they were original or significant.

Go ahead and quickly pull out your own ad. Seriously, go now and grab it or write it down. See if you can pass the "Well I would hope so" test and the "Who else can say that" test.

Think about what you're saying on your website. Can your competitors say the same thing you're saying? Usually they can because you're not being unique; you're not using a unique selling proposition. You don't have anybody helping you craft your message, which is the most important part of marketing.

The third of the three platitude tests is the "Cross-out/Write-in test." Here's the deal: can you put two ads, one of yours and one of your competitor's, right next to each other and cross out the name of your business and put your competitor's name in there and it basically be the same?

For most people, that's the way it works, even if it's a radio ad or a TV ad. You can basically take your name out, put your competitor's name in, and there's basically no difference. That's what we call the Cross-out/Write-in test.

Again, if you're doing this in your business, it means you're being boring. Yep, even you. It means you're not focusing on your message. All you care about is the medium.

Can you take your name and go put it on the competitor's ad and it's pretty much true? We see this in advertising all the time. That's why I ask, "What's the most important part of marketing?" The most important piece of marketing is your message.

Testimonials

Let's take this a step further. When we look at marketing, if you want to have a message that's free of platitudes, if you want a message that stands out, a message that attracts people, a message that makes people look at your business different, there's no better way than to use real testimonials from your reputation marketing program.

If you can take 5-stars and put it next to Mary Jane's name, who said, "Mike's Dry Cleaning was the best dry cleaning in town. Not only did they remove all the spots and stains, they put each individual piece of garment in its own plastic bag. Don't you hate when you have all those garments together in the same bag? At Mike's Dry Cleaning, they don't do that."

Let your customers write your advertising for you. Let your customers be your message in your marketing, and that's going to help you stand out.

Also, there's no better way to find out "what you're doing right" which will help you to continue to keep your customers happy. Find out what they value.

Another reason that reputation marketing is the most important piece of marketing other than your message is this: everything points to your online reputation now. Every single thing, whether it's the radio, the TV, the newspaper, Yellow Pages, online ad, magazines, billboards, or the back of a grocery store receipt.

Every survey shows that people go first to the Internet to check out a business. Maybe they're just looking for a phone number, or maybe they're looking for a location.

People go to the Internet, they type in your business name and the city you're in, which is one of the big changes Google made, and they instantly get a reputation report card.

All your other advertising and marketing dollars are either strengthened or hurt by reputation marketing.

If you're not paying attention to reputation marketing and you're doing any other form of advertising or media, you're wasting your money. People are just going to go online and look, and they're going to see a bad reputation, or they're going to see no reviews.

Reputation Marketing

The next thing is that people are looking for is your reputation.

The absolute most important part of marketing is your messaging, and it's our recommendation that you hire marketing professionals, such as us at Maverick, to help you craft your messaging so that you can have a congruent message that's not full of platitudes.

The great thing about using reputation marketing is you can use those 5-star reviews that come in as your marketing piece, and then you don't have those platitudes.

If we talk about the most important part of marketing, the absolute highest-level part of marketing today for businesses, it's to have a solid 5-star reputation on the Internet.

The most important part of your general marketing is your messaging. That being said, the most important thing of your online marketing is your online reputation. The reason your online reputation matters more than the messaging is because you can have a crummy message and people are still going to look at your reputation online. You can have stellar messaging and people are going to look at your reputation online. If your reputation online is not secured, the messaging doesn't matter anymore. True.

One thing people need to understand is that reviews are everywhere nowadays. Your business reviews are online. Your business reviews are in your marketing. Your business reviews are in all reference checks.

Do you recall from this book's introduction that I applied for an apartment and I gave them my eBay feedback score.? You know what the apartment managers did? They gave me the lease immediately. You know why? Because I had over 1,000 people say what a good honest guy I was. You can't fake that.

Your reputation, and your business's reputation is going to become more and more prevalent. I believe in the near future banks are going to use your business's online reputation as a basis for a loan approval.

I believe that credit cards and credit processors are going to use your business's online reputation as a basis for making a decision. They're going to use it in your reference checks.

Let me tell you, if you're not using a 5-star reputation in your marketing, it means you don't have a good reputation and people are going to start picking up on it. The only reason you'd be afraid to embrace this is if you have something to hide. Do you?

As more and more people start paying attention to reputation marketing, you're going to see how important it becomes to everybody. When we look at reputation marketing and we look at your reviews being everywhere and pointing to your business, it's not just Google, it's not just Yahoo, it's not just Bing or Angie's List or Yelp or City Square or City Search or Manta or Inside Pages or Yellow Pages or Dex; it's all these places.

There are hundreds and hundreds of websites online that are going to pool your reviews and point those towards your business because they're looking for content.

If you have bad reviews, they're going to pull those in and point those toward your Website and it's going to hurt you. Google is going out across the Internet using software "robots" and they're scouring the reviews and they're putting them at the bottom of your Google's local listing because they want to see what people are saying about you.

Reviews about you are absolutely everywhere and they are going to become more and more important in this day and age.

Since reviews are so important and since you have the ability to use the great ratings you receive in your marketing, don't you think it is really time to start making this the top priority in your business?

This is one of the main differences between smart business owners who are achieving incredible results online and those that are still wondering why they are not doing as well as they feel they should be.

The smart business owners are constantly building up their 5-star online reputation and then marketing that reputation to gain more customers, clients, and patients!

In the next chapter we are going to shift from good reviews to bad reviews and how to find out what people are saying "behind your back" online.

Mike LeMoine

More people speak out about what it's like to work with Mike and his company, MaverickWebMarketing.com

Dean Ford:
We fell very lucky to have found Maverick Web Marketing. Mike and his staff are first class. We have found the entire staff very reliable, knowledgeable and caring in terms of customer service. Mikes team has become an integral part of our business. Keep up the good work!!

Steve Sleeper:
I spent years looking for an Internet marketing company with the skill sets Maverick has. They take the time to get to know your needs first and are all about being of service - first and foremost. Maverick Web Marketing is truly an Internet marketing partner.

Jesse Erickson:
Mike is highly regarded in the Online Marketing industry - I have been to events and seen him teach

other marketers. He is a thought leader and you are lucky if you have the opportunity to work with him!

Chapter 7
What Are They Saying Behind My Back?

One of the questions we get all the time is, "How can I find out about my bad reviews?" I love hearing that because it means you understand the importance of reputation marketing.

There are numerous ways that you can find out about your bad reviews. Let me just tell you, the worst thing you can do is not care at all. A bad review can be out there haunting you. When we talk about negative reviews online, it's not fair, but in this day and age of the reputation and relationship economy, here's what happens:

You can have a disgruntled employee, you can have an employee who steals from you and you terminate, and any one of them can turn around and write you a negative review online. That negative review can haunt you for years, and there's nothing you can do about it.

Or that jerk customer who came in while already in a crappy mood, spilled his drink, yelled at the waitress, and ended up leaving you the bad review. Ugh…yeah, *that* guy.

It's very difficult in this day and age to remove negative reviews. You have to know about these things. A competitor can go and leave you a negative online review, and it can hurt you for years.

Search Out Your Reviews

You may not know about it unless you figure out ways to search for reviews. The first way you can look for your negative reviews is manually, with what we call *Manual Search Mode*.

Manual Search Mode is the absolute *worst* way to do this. Literally, what you're doing is going Website by Website, trying to find negative reviews. It's a waste of your time. Frankly, it's almost impossible to accomplish because there are so many websites where people can talk bad about your business that there's no way you can cover them all. It's absolutely not the way we recommend.

Another way you can learn about your reviews is to use Google alerts. Google alerts is a part of the Google search program where you can go and put keywords into an area. When those keywords pop up online, Google sends you an alert.

What would you do for Google alerts? You would put in your business name, your address, phone number, and anything relevant to you or your business so that if somebody posted something on the Internet relevant to that, you would get a Google alert. You can go to Youtube and search for "How to Set Up Google Alerts" to learn how to make this work.

This isn't a fail-proof option. The reason why is, the alerts don't pick everything up. Unless you've set the exact right keywords in Google alerts, it may not pick them up, which means that review can be out there haunting you for eternity.

The absolute best way is to use software like what we use at my company, Maverick Web Marketing. We have proprietary software that goes out and monitors all the top review sites for negative reviews.

It is imperative that our customers know what's being said about them on the Internet. It's imperative that if somebody leaves something negative about our clients, we can very quickly work on a response scenario to minimize the impact of that negative.

So many people are wrong when responding to a negative review. When you're responding to a negative review, you have to have a strategic way of doing it. I'll explain that soon. The best way to find out about negative reviews on the Internet is to use software like we use. It's proprietary, and that will allow you as a business owner to get notified any time there's a negative review online.

A Free Review Search for You

We can also go and search for negative reviews. If you go to RepMaverick.com, you can enter your business's information and you'll get a free report that shows you if you have negative reviews on the top sites out there.

RepMaverick.com is great to get an idea, but in the long run, you really need to be using software like ours where we can help you monitor all of those reviews. We monitor all of the top sites on a daily basis and we can instantly send you an email alert if something changes. Any monkey can create an online account and leave an unfair (or fair) review, but if you monitor them, you'll be prepared and have a plan of action, so it won't be something that creeps up on you later when it's too late to do anything about it.

In the next chapter we are going to talk about how to address negative reviews if you find them or if you get hit with one. This is a very important chapter because messing up here could cost you dearly in your quest to have great results with your online marketing.

More people speak out about what it's like to work with Mike and his company, MaverickWebMarketing.com

Kyle Battis:
I've been following Mike's work since I launched my own web marketing agency and I have always been impressed with the work that he and his team put out. He sets the bar high and leaves a great path for me and other local marketers to follow.

Gordon Mitchell, New Mexico Reverse Mortgage:
Mike and his crew are "head & shoulders" above everyone else when it comes to web marketing and using "outside the box" techniques to increase your marketing effectiveness. I had heard him give several public presentations that included some very unique strategies. Because of the information that he presented in those free public presentations, I met with him for a paid Consultation. The feedback and advice I received was invaluable. We are structuring some new campaigns that I am sure will be effective.

Thank you, Mike.

Clarence Fisher:

Maverick did an excellent job on our latest website project. They were knowledgeable, professional and fast! They took the time to ask questions and make sure I understood everything that needed to be done before beginning. Then they did more than they said they would do. I'm impressed. Thanks Mike. I will recommend to others.

Chapter 8
Help! I Have A Negative Review (or Many Negatives)

The question I get as soon as we talk about how to find negative reviews is, "How do I combat negative reviews?"

The first way to combat negative reviews is to be proactive before they ever happen. Here's what I mean: "The best defense against negative reviews is a very strong offense!"

The bottom line is it's very difficult to remove negative reviews off the Internet.

There are companies out there that claim they can, and occasionally they'll have some success. They'll usually bribe people with money to get the review removed.

Respond with the Positive

Most sites just don't allow you to remove negative reviews. It just doesn't happen. Honestly, the only thing you can do is combat the negative reviews with more positive reviews.

What that means is you've got to get more positive reviews piling in on a consistent basis so when somebody leaves you that negative, everything is in your favor. The percentages are in your favor.

Look at it this way: if you have one good review on the Internet and somebody goes and leaves you a negative review, now you have a 50 percent negative reputation online. That's gonna kill your business.

If you have nine positive reviews and somebody leaves you a negative one, now you have a 90 percent positive reputation. Do you see the difference? (We talked about this in another chapter, but I wanted to remind you how it worked.)

You want to minimize that impact of the negative review so much that it doesn't even really matter. The way you do that is to have a ton of positive reviews pouring in on a consistent basis so if you do get that negative review (which is inevitable nowadays) it will have less of an impact. It's a much smaller piece of the reputation pie.

Now that you know the harm one person having a bad day can do to your business, you'll understand why we work so hard to build your positive 5-star reputation online. By using our tools and strategies when you become a client of Maverick, we combat those negative reviews before they ever happen.

The next thing about combating negative reviews is this: you have to comment on them. In order to comment on your negative reviews, you have to find them, and in order to find them in time, you have to be using the right software.

Why is it so important? You don't want to find those reviews after it's too late. What we know is that most people who leave a negative review on the Internet really just want to be heard. The squeaky wheel gets the grease. They feel as if they were never understood.

So, to combat negative reviews, you have to know instantly when a negative review hits the Internet. The only way to do that is with software we use at Maverick that is proprietary and scans the entire Internet to look for those negative reviews. If you don't find them, it can be lingering out there and hurting you for years and you may never know it. But it's very important to find them so you can address them right away.

The Human Nature Aspect

A major mistake most people make when responding to negative reviews, is not being aware of human nature. Most of us, because we're small business owners who put a ton of time, effort, money, sweat, tears, blood and our entire soul into our business. As a result we want to go out and defend our business when somebody leaves a negative review.

That's human nature and it's also the absolute *worst way* to respond to a review.

What would you normally do if you read a negative review about your business? You'd tell them why they are wrong and all of the reasons why you're right.

They see your response as calling them a liar in public. And now you're having a very immature, very public, argument with the person who left you a negative review.

Most of the time, the people who leave you a negative review have nothing better to do than to fight you anyways.

Trust me when I say you don't want your negative review to show up as a Facebook post. Then you've got to fight it there, then it shows up on another website and another website. Before you know it, you're using all your time and energy that could be used to build your business trying to protect yourself from one review that's being posted over and over and in an online argument by a keyboard warrior.

Now, just for a second, consider the viewpoint of the third party who wasn't there, but is watching this bickering match online. You'll still look like the bad guy, even if you truly weren't at fault in the first place.

Next, what's going to happen via social media in our new economy? People are going to rally around the reviewer, and then you have basically a mob on your hands that you're trying to control.

What needs to happen instead? For starters, when you respond to a negative review, you're not responding to the person who left the review.

Your response needs to be written for the hundreds of people who are going to see that review at different times, the thousands, the tens of thousands, the millions of people over the lifespan of that review who are going to see it on the Internet.

You know what other people want to see? They want to see that you were reasonable. They want to see that you fixed the problem. People don't expect you to have an absolutely perfect reputation. They understand things happen. But when things happen, how do you respond to it? That's the measure of your business.

There's two scenarios: you can go and create a fight with somebody and go back and forth and basically slaughter your business's reputation online, or you can write a very strategic response for the person who left you a negative review, telling the rest of the world that you're a civil person, that you're going to take care of problems and that you're going to make it right.

No Oscar-worthy response needed; just an honest, kind, understanding response. A solution to the problem.

However, a word of caution: I once saw a restaurant owner who got a negative review and went on really trying to do good and responded to the negative review by saying, "We're so sorry that you had that experience with us. We don't operate that way. Next time you come in, we're going to give you a free meal. Just let us know."

What happened then? They got a whole slew of negative reviews.

Why? Because everybody wanted a free meal and the restaurant owner basically trained people that if you leave me a negative review, I'll give you a free meal. That guy ended up having to shut his review system down because he just couldn't handle it. You don't want to do that. You always want to handle problems offline. You want to handle problems out of the spotlight and in private.

A better response for that restaurant owner would have been, "We're so sorry to hear that you had a bad experience with us. We don't operate that way. The experience you had is unacceptable. Please contact me offline so we can discuss this further and allow me to make it right."

Everybody who sees that review sees this restaurant owner responded, he cares; he wants to fix the problem. *That's* what you want the world to know.

The last way that you respond to negative reviews and combat negative reviews is like the first given example; the best defense is a strong offense. You engrain reputation marketing into the culture of your business. So many people miss this. You as a business owner reading this understands how important reputation marketing is or you wouldn't be holding this book in your hands.

The rest of your team, the rest of your employees, the rest of your business doesn't know it. If you're an employee who is reading this book, it's your job to infuse the reputation marketing culture throughout the business.

Why is that important? This is important because every single person who has contact with a customer is responsible for that business's reputation in this new economy. You can have an employee having a bad day who affects one customer who leaves a review that affects your business for the rest of time. Ouch!

Maybe an employee just made a mistake. Maybe they didn't handle the situation properly. Basically, everybody in the organization has to have a culture of reputation marketing.

Training for Excellence

One of the things we do at Maverick, and I would highly recommend that everybody do, is to create a training program for your employees about the importance of reputation marketing. If you're a client of ours on our reputation system, we've already created this training program and given everyone access to it to teach and train your employees.

We actually have a small test that you can administer to your employees to make sure that they understand reputation marketing. They take the test, then the test is forwarded to you for your review.

Our video series teaches people the importance of reputation marketing. If you're not using something like we have, you'd better develop it on your own, be putting a training class together, and be making it part of your orientation or on-boarding of a new employee. It's important to make sure every single person in your organization understands how important your business's reputation truly is, and the ways to protect it.

What you'll see is the businesses that have the best reputation have the best culture, and they teach and talk about reputation marketing on a continual basis.

Why do you think companies like Amazon and Zappos have such stellar customer service? It's because they've infused reputation marketing into their entire organization so every single person knows how to handle the customer.

Why do they do that? Because reviews on the Internet for companies like eBay and Zappos and Amazon are the lifeblood of those businesses. It is the lifeblood of your business too!

If they start getting negative reviews on products or word starts getting out about horrible customer service, they will lose hundreds of millions of dollars. The same thing goes for your business. Don't think it doesn't affect you.

Brendan Bouchard is a peer in our industry, and he has a great line that I love which says: *"Don't let your small business make you small-minded."*

Basically, don't think just because you're not Amazon or Zappos or eBay that this doesn't affect you. It absolutely does. If you want to combat negative reviews, again, you have to have more positive reviews than you do negative.

You have to create that strong offense, which is the absolute best defense. You have to have a way to find reviews and respond to them in the appropriate way as soon as possible. You have to create and infuse a reputation marketing culture into your business.

In the next chapter I am going to talk to you about the number one thing I am sure you are dying to know: How to get more 5-star reviews!

Mike LeMoine

More people speak out about what it's like to work with Mike and his company, MaverickWebMarketing.com

Nehal Kazim:
Maverick is exceptionally good at proactively marketing and growing businesses. Mike and his team really know their stuff and I consult with them frequently about proven strategies I can implement in my business.

I highly recommend Maverick!

Jamie Thompson:
The team at Maverick web Marketing are amazing! They have recently done our website for my flower shop and I am so very pleased with what they have done. They know what they are doing and I am seeing such great results. Thank you Maverick Team!

Greg Purdy:
Mike LeMoine knows his stuff! Having a basic understanding of what you want is one thing -

Knowing how to achieve results is something altogether different. Maverick Web Marketing not only knows what works, they know how and WHY it works. They know why things you're doing are not currently working, and they know how to make corrections. Forget trial and error - Your money will be far better spent hiring Maverick Web Marketers to do it right the first time!

Chapter 9
The Million Dollar Question

When asked about negative reviews, I like to say the best defense is a strong offense. I know I'm beating a dead horse here but that is truly the long-term definitive answer.

If we've talked about how to avoid negative reviews, the next obvious question is: "How do I get more positive reviews?" If the best defense against negative reviews is getting positive reviews, how do you get more positive reviews?

Ask for them.

Asking for Reviews

There are a number of ways to ask. The first thing is you have to have a system. That's why we call it reputation marketing, because it's a system that you have to put into place for your marketing.

Getting reviews is not like, "I'm going to wake up and get some reviews today," and then you can forget about it. It needs to be an ongoing process because it takes time. You don't want to try to get reviews once it's too late. You want to always be working on this.

You *always* want to be working on your reputation. Tell me, when is the time that your reputation on the Internet or anywhere else doesn't matter? Between 9 and 10am and again between 2 to 5am. No!

Putting Systems in Place

The correct answer is *never*. You don't ever want to slack off. You therefore have to put systems in place. We'll take it from the basics, and we can move up to the advanced.

One of the things you need to do is forecast. You don't want to assume that everything is going to be okay. What you're forecasting is that at some point you're going to get a negative review.

You better start now in building that reputation-marketing system so that you are the most protected and most prepared if that ever happens. Actually "when," not "if."

Remember, another great thing about using reputation marketing and having that system in place is you're always going to have good marketing material.

From a very basic standpoint, if we're talking about a system, a very basic system would tell somebody after you've done business with them, "Can you please give me a review on Google?" That is actually better than nothing if you know you have good customer service.

Here's the problem with that, though. Eventually, you're going to ask somebody to leave you a review who you're not 100% sure if it'll be positive or not. You're going to find out there was something wrong once it's too late, and you're actually going to create negative reviews that way.

Yep. You probably didn't see that one coming.

We certainly don't want to be putting more negative reviews on the Internet. It would be the equivalent as if you owned a restaurant and somebody came up to the counter and said he wasn't happy with the food, you wouldn't stand up on the counter and yell to everyone, "This guy's not happy. Let me tell you about it."

No, you take care of the problem and keep it quiet to move your business forward. You wouldn't want that person to go and tell their family and friends that they had a bad experience. You'd want them to say, "Things didn't go well, but they made it right."

We feel the same way about the Internet. We don't want to send everybody to Google, Yahoo!, Bing or to any of the other review sites. We don't want to just send them there, because we don't know what they're going to put.

We want to make sure that if they're going there, they had a great experience. If they didn't, we need to fix the problem first. We don't need to have them go leave a review. We need to go fix the problem.

A Triage Page

That's why we don't really recommend just sending them to Google or any of the other sites. If they had a problem, it doesn't give you an opportunity to fix it.

When we build our systems for reputation marketing, we actually build a review "triage" page. What is a review triage page? It's a page that we send people to so we can get their opinion, just like if you were doing a survey at your business. It's an online internal survey to see what their opinion of your service was.

When we do that, if they had a negative opinion, or a negative experience, we immediately alert the business owner so they can fix the problem.

If they had a good experience, then we'll direct them and ask them to please leave a review on whatever site we're trying to build reviews on.

This is so important because, number one, we're able to separate the people who aren't happy from the people who are. We're able to instantly help the people who aren't happy and be able to fix the problem. Once the problem is fixed, that's the point where the business owner asks them to go leave a review.

If they were happy, we can then enable them to go and leave a review on one of the other sites, but we at least know the review is most likely going to be positive.

> **Caution:** When we're talking about reputation marketing, we want to do everything "white hat."

In the online world, "black hat" is the sneaky tricky stuff that will get you in trouble. "White hat" is the stuff that's totally legit.

We don't ever want to do anything "black hat". This could get you and your business in a lot of trouble.

Reviews and your reputation are far too important to risk using these bad tactics, tactics like posting fake reviews or paying people to leave reviews or any of that stuff. That happens all the time and I'll get into that a little bit more later, but you want to avoid that at all costs!

We don't ever ask people to leave us a 5-star review. We simply ask people for their honest review, and here's why: if somebody is going to be negative, we want their honest opinion so you can fix the problem.

If somebody's not honest with you, you can never fix a problem you don't know you have. On the same token, if they've had a great experience, we want them to articulate that experience in their own words. We don't ever want to sway people, so we just simply ask for their review and feedback.

That's so important to know.

You don't want to incentivize people to leave a certain review. The only thing you can incentivize people for is their time, because you're asking people to go above and beyond to take time out of their lives to help you with their feedback.

You can incentivize them for their time but be cautious. Never incentivize someone for leaving you a positive or negative review. You can say at most, "I will give you a coupon for taking the time to leave me an honest review," something like that.

Again, please hear me: never pay for a positive review and never incentivize people to leave you any positive reviews. Simply incentivize them for their time and take whatever you get. If it's a negative fix the problem. If it's a positive, help move them to a site where it would be beneficial to you and your business if they leave you a review there.

A lot of times, another reason to capture that review before you ask them to go to another site is so you can help them and instruct them on how to leave that review, because a lot of people simply don't know how to leave reviews.

Unfortunately, most of the review systems make it pretty complicated because they want to avoid spam or fake reviews. So, there's a level of learning that has to occur on a lot of these sites. If you did not capture that positive review and then leave them instructions on how to leave it, chances are it's going to be much more difficult for them to leave reviews. You can see now that if you have a system in place to get people to go to a survey page and take a survey on their experience with you, how beneficial that is to your business. You could either fix that problem or assist them with putting that good review on the Internet and that's so important!

Getting Them There

How do you get people to your survey page? That's another great question.

Once you've built this survey page, or whatever your survey system looks like, how do you enter people into your system? There are a lot of different ways to be able to get people into your system and we will cover that in the next chapter.

Mike LeMoine

More people speak out about what it's like to work with Mike and his company, MaverickWebMarketing.com

Scott Cunningham:

Mike & the Maverick Marketing team are true local marketing rock stars! I consider Mike as one of my top online local marketing mentors. I appreciate Mike for his depth and breadth of marketing knowledge as well as his character. He has earned my trust and business. I look forward to working with Mike for a long time. I would highly recommend Maverick Marketing for your local marketing needs.

David Crum:

Mike and the gang at Maverick handle all of the Facebook and video marketing for our law firm, New Mexico Legal Group. Not only great services and products, but really fun people to work with. Keep up the great work guys!

Steven Nelson, Hot Tubs Albuquerque:
We have been using Maverick Web for almost a year and the results are outstanding! We were ranked first on most searches unusually fast and we have stayed there. Our customer traffic is up so high that we already need to expand our showroom. Our new customers used to come in very standoffish and now come in expecting to explore the different spas. It's like they already know us before they begin shopping. If you work with these guys expect to do your part getting the website rolling then stand back and watch your business grow.

Jason Bell:
The team at Maverick marketing are a superb group of people that have a 'givers' heart. We had a 20-minute brainstorming session on areas I needed help with, and they willingly provided their time and knowledge as we found great solutions to the issues I was facing in growing my business. I highly recommend the Maverick team for any future business consulting. Thank you all!

Chapter 10
Getting People to Take Action

Let's now get into the methods of asking people to go to your survey page. There's a lot of different ways to do it, from simple to very complex, from moderately effective to super effective.

Start by thinking of everywhere that you have contact with customers and how you drive them there.

Let's talk email. First off, you could actually put your review survey page in the bottom of your email with a sentence that says something such as, "Please rate your experience with us," "click here," or something along those lines.

You could also put it in your email signature. Or, include it in an email auto responder series so that when somebody buys your service, product, or does business with you, you send them an email that automatically asks them to help with your survey.

You've probably seen this type of thing before from hotel chains, mechanics, and other serviced-based businesses. A lot of people are doing this in the bigger markets, but not so much in the small business arena.

The technology and the affordability of it weren't there in the past. We've been able to change that at Maverick and make it very affordable for all businesses to have a system in place to help with their reputation marketing and getting more 5-star reviews.

We leverage very high-end technology to be able to help small businesses do this. As a result, our clients are doing phenomenally well with their reputation marketing which is leading to greater client/customer acquisition, retention, and more money!

Another very common method is to put your invitation on a receipt. On your receipt, you could ask your customers/clients/ patients/patrons to please visit your survey page and leave a review. If you invoice your clients, another great place to put them is on your invoice. Are you making a list? Taking notes? You should be!

By far, the most popular way of doing it is by handing out a special review card. We have people who hand out business cards that say, "Please take the time to leave us a review." Even those cards will sometimes say what you are willing to give them for taking the *time* to leave a review.

This helps incentivize people to take that time. Again, please know you're only enticing them for the time; you are not enticing them for any type of specific review. It's very important to understand that.

Postcards are also popular. I like the postcard method better than the business card method because they're bigger and easier to handle. That postcard is directing people to your review survey page to be able to leave you that review.

Direct mail is absolutely fantastic for this. If you have a mailing list of people who have done business with you, you can send them a letter or a postcard in the mail. You can reach out to people to get those reviews, once you have your survey page.

Two Review Styles

There are really two styles when it comes to the review. There are the people who you're doing business with now, and there are also the people who you've done business with in the past. And we've got to be able to reach out to those people too. Hold that thought, we'll come back to that.

Another method (and probably my favorite method) for getting reviews—this method works if you have a higher gross margin on a product or service where you can afford to do this—is to send out a thank you card to your customer, and inside the thank you card, you ask for their review.

Now, I know that sounds time consuming. Again, here at Maverick, we have systems in place where all you have to do is enter the information in an online form.

It literally takes about 15 seconds and you can then have a real card created, put in an envelope, stamped with a real stamp, and sent to your customer. When the receive the card, they get excited seeing a real card and feel more inclined to go ahead and leave you that review. This has been extremely successful, and it accomplishes a couple of things.

It's appreciation marketing, which I could write a whole other book on. Most businesses don't thank their customers, which is ridiculous. You're thanking your customer and you're asking them to take the time to leave a review. Many times, these reviews are even better because you just sent the customer a thank you card, which nobody is doing. So, that's another great way to get people into the system.

So, let's talk about that customer list of people who have done business with you before. They're not in front of you right now. There are a couple of great ways to reach them. The best way is direct mail. I'm a very big believer in the thank you-card system. You could take a list, and send them all a thank you card, while also asking for a review.

Again, you don't have to do it through any system. You can go get a box of cards and write them all out by hand, which is nice and personal. However, if your list is in the hundreds, or a thousands, you may not have the time or ability to sit down and do that. That's why at Maverick we have systems in place to automate that entire process for you.

Another way would be direct mail. Can you write a letter and send it out to everyone who has done business with you thanking them, asking them for a review? Absolutely.

Another way to do it would be email. If you have your customers' email addresses, you can do email blasts, asking them to visit your review page and leave you a review.

So, those are a few ways for you to get the word out about your review page. Those are the ways you learn from your customers and past customers what their experience doing business with you was like.

Hopefully, they've had a good experience. Then we can instruct them on how to leave a review on those sites.

Responding to Positive Reviews

It is very important that you respond to reviews. In this book we spend quite a bit of time on responding to a negative review. But it is equally as important to respond to positive reviews too. You want your responses to be personalized. Don't just copy and paste a generic "thank you." This person just took time to say something amazing about you, your team, your product, your service, your company. Do them the courtesy of giving a damn and responding to their review.

Also, much like negative responses remember that thousands and tens of thousands of people will be seeing these responses in the future. If you are personable and caring in your responses this will continue to help you build trust and credibility for you and your company.

Others will see the reviews and the responses, and they will be much more apt to do business with you. Another cool thing, responding to reviews creates a lot more digital real-estate if you need to push a negative review down. It also ads a lot of content to each positive review too, which makes it more powerful and credible.

The bottom line as we wrap this up, is it's all about systems. You have to have a system in place, or you'll never do it. If you don't have a system in place—if you don't have a process in place—then you will only do this when you think about reviews. You can't leave this to chance. It's way too important. What we have to do is be able to move this ship forward and be able to have a system to get reviews taken care of, and make sure it's a habit—much like coming into a room and turning on the lights or going to the bank to make a deposit.

Reviews really *are* that important. If you're not protecting your reputation, then you're not going to have to worry about those bank deposits for a long time because it's not going to matter. Your business will not make enough money if you're not paying attention to reputation.

Systematize this process using a program that works for you. If you need help, feel free to get a hold of us here at Maverick and learn what has helped us, and our clients. No need to recreate the wheel. You can visit us at MaverickWebMarketing.com

The bottom line is, you don't have to do it with us, but you do have to get something in place. Your business needs to be able to have a reputation marketing program to assist you in getting those positive 5-star reviews that will move your business forward, attract more customers, and help you make more money.

In the next chapter we will cover what websites you need to be paying attention to when it comes to getting your reviews online.

Mike LeMoine

More people speak out about what it's like to work with Mike and his company, MaverickWebMarketing.com

Andy Warren:

Four or five years ago Mike sent an email to all the painters in town telling them they are "dumb" because his fake paint company "Duke City Painting" was ranked higher than them on Google. He said he would work with one paint company and put them on the top of the Google search list. I hired him first and have been working with Mike (and I have been on top of Google) since then. Mike and his team are the front runners on the internet marketing scene. He is always calling or emailing to let me know what has changed and how we can take advantage of it. I have and will continue to recommend Maverick Web Marketing to anyone who has a business and needs internet exposure.

Anne LeMoine:

Great group that are very hardworking! They were very patient and worked with us to make the end result exactly what we wanted. Thanks for a great time guys!

Marshall LeMoine:

Shot more than 200 videos over 4 days with Maverick Web Marketing, and everything turned out great. Michael, Sean and the rest of the staff with very helpful and true professionals. Thanks for all your hard work and time!

Mike Wong:

We went to film videos and working with the team was awesome. Long hours, making sure things were perfect.... definitely made it worth our trip! Great guys.

Chapter 11
Where Do Reviews Need to Go Online?

Which websites do you need to focus on as far as reviews go?

That's a great question. It's important to know that it really depends on the industry you're in for us to determine which websites matter, so what I'm going to do is start with some of the big ones and then we'll kind of go industry specific.

The fact is, there are a ton of sites out there that review your business and you need to make sure that your business is getting reviews on the sites that matter to you. First, the broad sites like Google, Yahoo, and Bing and then the other specific sites like maybe Angie's List, Zomato, or TripAdvisor.

How do you do all this? Well, you've got to have a strategic plan. First thing's first. Always start with Google. It's by far the most important. Once you've done that on Google, we then rotate that same strategy over to Yahoo and Bing or possibly an industry-specific site.

You'll always need to analyze and look at your reputation marketing strategy. You're always plotting and forecasting where the next place is where you're going to work on your reputation. This builds a very cohesive and comprehensive reputation marketing program showcasing your business's 5-star reputation across the entire Internet.

That's really what you want to do when it comes to getting people to leave reviews, plan which review sites you want to focus on because those are the ones that matter most at the time, then move on to the next site when things are going well. Remember this is a marathon, not a sprint.

Clearly you need to get moving with some force, but you have to maintain it and continue it. Reputation marketing is not one of those programs that you do for a while and then stop.

The Internet has made it where reputation marketing is vital for your success and it will always be an ongoing program. Much like you cannot run your business without electricity, you're going to have a very hard time being successful, sustainable and continue your business if you're not using reputation marketing and if you don't have a reputation marketing system or program in place.

As you put your system in place make sure you map out which sites you need to be focused on first for your business to build its reviews on. This is an important step to figure out to ensure that you maximize the value of each and every positive review that comes into your system.

In the next chapter, I will expand on having an employee education system in place to ensure that your team knows about the importance of 5-star reviews and the impact just a single negative review can have on your business.

Mike LeMoine

More people speak out about what it's like to work with Mike and his company, MaverickWebMarketing.com

Larry Espinoza:
Not only are the gang from Maverick a team players, they are honest and efficient. Not only do they do what they say they are going to do... they explain the process and communicate with you through out. Thank you Maverick!

Michael Barker:
Have personally worked with Maverick to improve my own LLC, and am still reaping the benefits. We appreciate them very much - very recommended!

Mike LeMoine

Chapter 12
Making Sure Your Team Is Up to Speed!

Another thing we need to touch on, and we've touched on it a little bit already, is this question: "How do I instill this into my employees or team?"

Three main ways exist that you accomplish this.

Number one is training. You have to educate and train them. Maybe you make this part of your employee orientation, or you have a special brochure or pamphlet you hand out that you introduce to everybody. Or possibly you bring it in to your employee training. No matter how you introduce it, your employees must be trained and understand how important reputation marketing is to your business.

Our clients get an entire portal that their employees can go in and have us teach them the importance of reputation marketing, then their employees take a test on it to make sure they understand. It's that important that we built out an entire training portal just for businesses to be able to get their employees trained and understanding reputation marketing.

Take Action Yourself

Another way to ensure your employees get this is *action*. What I mean by that is you've got to set the example. You've got to show them you're seriously committed to a reputation marketing program.

So often, entrepreneurs get excited and want to move forward and do things. They get their employees on board and then things just fizzle out because they don't follow through. So, a major component of a successful reputation marketing program includes follow up and follow through.

You have to show your employees you're committed to this because if you're not committed, they're not going to be committed. No surprise there.

Employee Incentives for Reviews

I'm a very big advocate of incentives for your employees for online reviews and in helping orchestrate a successful online review. Why is that?

Well, in the reputation and relationship economy where having a 5-star reputation is so important to your business, it is well worth giving your employees some type of compensation, recognition, or both, for helping to receive 5-star reviews from customers.

Think of this as an insurance policy for your business long term. Whether it's a gift card, or a few extra bucks in their paycheck as a bonus, any one of these things is going to be super helpful in getting your employees on board.

Another idea is to run a contest for your employees over 30 days and whichever employee drives the most positive 5-star reviews gets a special bonus dinner out with their spouse, a movie, a trip. Anything you can do to incentivize your team, your employees, to help orchestrate this 5-star reputation marketing program is absolutely vital.

You're not always going to have the opportunity to interact with customers on a regular basis, it's probably going to be your team doing it, and if you and your team aren't on the same page, if you're not teaching your team, helping and instructing them, you're really doing yourself and your business a disservice.

In order to get your team on board, you're going to have to train them. You're going to have to test them. You're going to have to teach them. You're going to have to lead from the front and you're going to have to incentivize them!

That's why companies that work with us really appreciate our programs because we're able to help them plan out and organize so much of this. Again, you don't have to work with us, but you should be doing this with your team and with your employees on a regular basis.

In the next chapter, I'm going to dive into some tips and tricks to help you in this new economy.

Mike LeMoine

More people speak out about what it's like to work with Mike and his company, MaverickWebMarketing.com

Chris Leake:

Top notch marketing experts! That's what I have to say about the team at Maverick. They worked with us on a large video project a little while back, and they were very skilled, knowledgeable, friendly, and they went the extra mile.

I have known Mike for several years now. Any time I need help or insight with marketing a local business, Maverick has been my go-to for as long as I've known them. These guys know their stuff inside and out, they have a wealth of experience working with many different types of businesses, and they stay on top of the constantly changing trends on the internet.

I give them my highest recommendation! When it comes to marketing for a local business, in my opinion there's no one better.

Mike LeMoine

Chapter 13
A Few Last Tips

We've talked about many ways to market reviews, but I always get asked about other ways one can market reviews.

Reviews are great to put on the back of business cards, and yet, so many people leave this space blank.

Having all these reviews—having a 5-star reputation— now gives you a lot of marketing material to put in those spots that are usually blank. So, the back of business cards—or even the front—are extremely good. I actually like the idea of putting a review on the front of business cards, and your information on the back because that review is going to catch someone's eye, which is going to want to make them contact you. Being able to put these reviews on your website—every page of your website—should have your reviews, and your reputation marketing status clearly defined. Putting those on your website is absolutely huge and critical to attracting more buyers and more customers, prospects, or patients via your website.

In fact, you should have reviews as part of your main website menu. I still see businesses using "testimonials" in the menu. Change that to "reviews" and more people will actually go there. People trust reviews far more than testimonials!

Whether it's radio, TV, newspaper, yellow pages, magazines, or billboards, using that 5-star reputation you've earned, and being able to put those on different ads and different media, really strengthens your business's position in the marketplace.

Another great place to be able to use reviews is on YouTube. Film your reviews. You can film yourself reading written reviews of what the customer said about you. Then, put them out on YouTube so your customers can see those reviews and what people are saying.

Take those YouTube videos and embed them into your website as testimonial videos so people can see what your customers are saying about you. Be proud of your reviews and showcase them!

The opportunity to use these reviews goes on and on and on. You can put them in your brochures. You can do proposals. If you do proposals, you can create two or three sheets of positive 5-star reviews and just attach that to every single proposal.

I promise you, your competitors aren't doing these things. They're not thinking outside of the box. They're not thinking strategically about their reputation. If you do, you have a phenomenal advantage over them.

Think about getting a proposal from three different companies. One company has three pages of positive 5-star reviews talking about their business and the other companies are just asking for money. Who are you going to go with? Well, you're definitely going to go with the company that has those positive 5-star reviews.

Think of the last time you were "pitched." Are you more likely to go with a company who has their ducks in a row—and a big stack of reviews to prove it—or any Joe Schmoe who thinks they've earned your business just by showing up for the meeting?

When you're thinking about how to use these reviews, there are so many ways that we just can't cover in this book. But I encourage you to look at the ways you're marketing and figure out how you can integrate those 5-star reviews into everything you're doing.

I'm a very big believer in sending out cards to different people; so, another great way to be able to expose your 5-star reputation is to send out cards to potential clients.

For example, let's say you're a business that meets people face to face. Then, you have to send a thank you card after a meeting. Well, this is a perfect opportunity to be able to embed reviews into that thank you card.

You say it was nice to meet them. Thank them for taking the time to meet with you. Then, on the inside, on the blank part of the card, you just have a ton of positive reviews so people know that you're somebody they can trust, you're somebody who is serious about business, and you're somebody that other people spend money with.

Nobody wants to be the first one into a market. Nobody wants to be the "guinea pig." If you can show people that other people have made this move and other people have had positive experiences, you're breaking down a lot of the barriers that normally are there in creating a sale.

You really need to pay attention to the opportunity to use these reviews. Here's another idea. If you send anything in boxes, being able to print those reviews right on the boxes so customers and everybody who handles those boxes gets to see it. If you're a pizza company, for example, a pizza delivery, or a pizza restaurant, you can put reviews right on the boxes!

If you do eCommerce and you're mailing stuff out, you can put reviews right on the boxes. If you're a company that sends things via mail, you can create a printed sheet and put that in the box and send that out. There are so many opportunities around you to use positive 5-star reviews. Just look for them!

If you have a brick and mortar business, you can blow those reviews up into posters and plaster your business with them so that when people come in, all they see are positive responses about what other clients have said about you.

You could take all those reviews, put them on your website, put a buy button or a phone number, and you're going to convert tons of people just because you have your 5-star reputation.

Dan Kennedy talks about money in the bank now, and money in the bank in the future. I really believe that reputation marketing is filling not only your current bank account, but it is really filling your future bank account to make things very, very successful for you.

Always be on the lookout for how you can integrate these 5-star reviews into every single piece of your online marketing, your offline marketing, and any marketing that you're doing.

The Social Media Aspect

We've touched on it before, but let's talk more about social search, how reviews matter in social media, and how you can integrate reviews into social media.

The easiest is just to take those reviews and post them, whether you're posting them on Facebook, YouTube, Twitter or LinkedIn. We've gone over some strategies like that already, but what you're going to see is these social media sites becoming more and more prevalent and looking for opportunities to get reviews about your business.

Again, they're going to be integrated into the social search. When people are looking for you on social media, reviews are going to be integrated. When people are looking for you on the Internet, part of the algorithm is going to become your social search profile with reputation marketing. So, what the social media sites say about you is going to dictate and affect where your business ranks online.

The other thing to remember is these social media sites have so many people interacting with them that if you're not paying attention to your social search, and your reputation online, it's going to hinder your business because more and more people are going to continue to get on social media.

Get on every platform you can to get reviews. As these platforms mature and change, you already have that positive 5-star reputation working for you, helping you and, putting you light years ahead of your competition in all these arenas.

These are just a few ideas to help you out. We have so many more ways that we help our clients market with their 5-star reviews, this this will get your brain turning with the possibilities.

In the next chapter we are going to do a deep dive into the new economy and show you how it really came to be and where it is going long term so you can be ready!

Mike LeMoine

More people speak out about what it's like to work with Mike and his company, MaverickWebMarketing.com

Tony Sandlin, Professional Balloon Ride Operators:
The entire team is awesome to work with. Mike Came to our annual meeting at Balloon Fiesta and gave an awesome presentation of Social Media! So awesome we are exploring the possibility of using them again!

Bouncing Buddies:
We had the pleasure of meeting the Maverick Web Marketing team in New Orleans last week. After a short conversation with these guys I knew it was a good fit for us. I've gotten more training out of a 2-hour phone call with them than anything else we've ever done. Excited about moving forward with this team.

PDR ABQ:
Maverick's review system worked great! In a year we went from 1 review to over 40 5-star reviews on google. I highly recommend their service!

Venessa Chavez:
I have had the pleasure of working with Mike and Lori LeMoine. They are a power couple who love to empower small business owners to take their business to the next level. Their recent review of our recruiting video left us inspired to take our work to the next level. With their help we have a solid commercial which has helped us recruit the high caliber professionals we want on our team! Thanks it has been a pleasure working with you! We will be back!

Chapter 14
The New Economy

I've talked a lot about the new economy, but I really want to address it here in detail. What I mean by the new economy on the Internet is the *reputation and relationship economy.* That matters tremendously because in this new economy, reputation and relationships are the digital "word of mouth."

When businesses really started to get online and get on the Internet, they would build a website and the website was, basically, a digital brochure for their business.

That was acceptable for a while, but then we moved into the social media economy. The social media economy is really businesses having to move from a static brochure site into interacting with their customers. It used to be that with static brochure sites that people would just come, get their information, maybe they'd buy or call you and that was it.

People are all very social in nature, so what happened to us as human beings on the Internet, is we yearned for that social interaction. Because of that, social media sites like Facebook, Twitter, LinkedIn, and YouTube were born.

We all wanted that social media interaction and so what you saw were businesses having to make this shift into social media. Now, not all businesses have done it, but social media is still absolutely imperative because you *have* to be interacting with your customers.

Following the rise of the social media giants, we all started interacting, and people got very comfortable with that. So, we then moved into the new era (where we are now) of the reputation and relationship economy, what we call the "new economy."

The reason why is as social media built up, it was natural for us to share our experiences with our friends and family via social media and digital platforms. People realized all this, which lead to review sites being thought about. People did want to express their opinions and feelings and needed venues to allow for that. And that is how review sites came to be.

That's why this new economy is so important to participate in. You have to have a good reputation with your customers, and if you're not doing that through the use of social media and through the use of reputation marketing, you're not allowing your business to thrive online and then thrive offline like it should. Which begs the question, "Are you in your own way?" If you are, get the heck out!

A quick point about the reputation and relationship economy is in order though. Unfortunately, one bad review can hurt your business very, very badly because you can't control it.

If you don't know about that review, if you don't know where it's been posted, if you're not paying attention, hundreds of thousands of people over the course of time can see that review and make buying decisions based on that. They can, and will, make the decision not to buy from you.

The Power of Information

In this economy, this information is front and center. People are talking. People are sharing. People are interacting. Interestingly 85% of people—some studies cite upwards of 93%—trust online reviews as much as if a friend told them. We don't all have to be buddies to trust what somebody else says. We trust blindly other Internet users, other strangers who we've never met, because of a review platform and a star. In the reputation and relationship economy, it's vital for us to be paying attention to all these things so that not only can we survive, we can absolutely go on and thrive!

Into the Future

The next logical question about all this new economy, online reputation marketing, and reviews on the Internet is this: "What is the future going to be like?"

Well, the future is going to be everlasting. It's green. You need to think of a way that people can get information *before* they make a buying decision, because that's always going to be very, very popular.

Everybody goes to the Internet to get a question answered, or a pain relieved, or a problem solved. Now sometimes, that pain could be boredom and they're going to the Internet to watch funny cat videos.

However, when it comes to businesses, people go online for more information. People go to the Internet so they can get questions answered, so they can find out before they spend their hard-earned money.

If people can go to the Internet and research a business's reputation, and research the way a business does business before they spend their money with them, that's always going to be very, very popular. So that's one reason it's going to be everlasting.

Another reason it's going to be everlasting is businesses are being built around reputation. Just look at Angie's list. Look at Yelp. Look at some of these other sites. These are people who are making some a lot of money off of reputation. And your business needs to be rewarded for that.

Google is making money off reputation, and so are Yahoo! and Bing. Everybody realizes there's money to be made in the small business/local business market and they're going to base a lot of this on reputation.

They can get interaction, and if you can get interaction you can also get buy in. Then when you get that buy in, you can show companies how important it is for them to participate in your service.

I don't believe that the reputation or relationship economy is ever going to go away, and there's always the probability of new forms and new variances. The bottom line though is your reputation online will always play a vital and key role in the success of your online marketing program. This is the new standard by which your business is going to be judged and what you're going to see—it's already happening—all these reviews and the reputation strategies are going to be integrated into social media. Facebook is already doing this. YouTube already has the thumbs up button.

More and more companies are going to integrate reputation and social media as they mix the medium and the media to give the users a better experience.

What you're going to see are social media companies starting to pay attention to the online reviews and integrating them into social media. What that means to a business is that no matter where somebody is on the Internet, your reputation is going to be front and center.

And if you are in the business of good customer service and treating people right, this is great news!

It's absolutely vital to you as a business owner to pay attention to this because your reputation is already all over the Internet, and it matters to your potential customers, which means as a business your reputation better matter to you.

Not only now, but even more so moving into the future. You're going to be behind the curve if you don't have a good reputation or if you don't have an absolutely 5-star great reputation.

You know Wayne Gretzky talks about "I don't skate where the puck has been. I skate where the puck is going." That's why businesses need to jump on this early and see where the puck is going.

Know what reputation marketing is. Business owners who see where this is going and jump on the curve early are going to be mega successful compared to those businesses that don't take action, don't pay attention, or that choose not to be cutting edge with a strategy that's going to be around for a very, very, very long time.

Think about this. If you had the opportunity to jump in a DeLorean and go back five to 10 years and figure out search engine optimization. If you took action five to 10 years ago and your business stayed on top of Google no matter what, wouldn't you want to be there? Absolutely!

Where would you be at this point in time with those sorts of results? How would that have changed your life? More time with the kids? More vacations? How would that business success change your current life situation?

Well, it's the same thing with reputation marketing. You have the opportunity to position your business as the authority and the expert to gain reviews so that by the time your competition figures this out you're going to be many reviews ahead.

You're going to have your business information and your 5-star reputation in so many places, they will never catch up with you. That's why I say with complete confidence, the first business to understand reputation marketing is going to win at this game in their industry.

That's why the future of reputation marketing and online reviews is going to be extended into infinity and that's why, again, as a business you can't afford to have a short-term mindset when it comes to reputation marketing.

You really need to be looking at your long-term results, your long-term goals, and know that as long as you're in business you better be managing, protecting, and increasing your 5-star reputation. As long as you're going to be on the Internet, you're going to have to be doing this as well because this stuff is not going to go away.

77% of consumers think that reviews older than 3 months aren't relevant (Source: BrightLocal, Local Consumer Review Survey 2017)

In the paragraph above I said how this game will never end. That reviews are around to stay. Take a look at that stat from BrightLocal. If you are not getting new reviews you reviews are viewed as not relevant after just three months. Bottom line, you can't rest on your laurels and think that just because you have some good reviews you are done. Your reputation must become part of your DNA inside of how your business operates. It must be something that is automatic. It must be on the radar at all time. This is why having a reputation system is so important. You need a machine that is always working for you to build, protect, and market your reputation online!

Remember that we are here to help you with your reputation marketing and all aspects of your online marketing. We have many ways we can help your business. Just reach out to us at:

MaverickWebMarketing.com.

Mike LeMoine

The Wrap-Up

As a wrap up to this book, I first want to thank you for taking the time to read it. We will be updating this book to keep it current with what is going on in the world of reviews.

Remember, as you embark on looking and building your reputation program that each piece is essential and serves a vital purpose. That is why I took the time to break it down in the book.

I know that because you read this book you are at the forefront of your industry and you are really understanding that the world is a different place. I congratulate you on gaining the knowledge that you need to be successful online.

As you know because I mentioned it several times in the book my company Maverick Web Marketing has many strategic ways we help our clients to get more 5-star reviews online and also turn those reviews into epic marketing.

Remember that when it comes to building your online reputation and putting a system into place that it is like the quote about planting a tree:

> "The best time to plant a tree was 20 years ago, the second-best time is now."

Therefore:

> "The best time to build and start a reputation marketing program and system was years ago, the second-best time is right now."

Contact us and we can help you make this happen!

I would love to have the opportunity to earn your business by helping you with your online marketing. If you would like to learn more about us, you can visit us at:

MaverickWebMarketing.com

You can just use the contact tab if you would like to reach us to discuss your online marketing more.

Thanks again for reading.

~ Mike

Made in the USA
Columbia, SC
12 August 2019